3 0132 0

D1576797

1 3 OCT 2010

Odes for Oldies

Illustrations by Naomi Tipping

Clive Whichelow

summersdale

Summersdale Publishers Ltd
46 West Street
Chichester
West Sussex
PO19 1RP
UK

www.summersdale.com

Printed and bound by CPI Group (UK) Ltd, Croydon, CR0 4YY

ISBN: 978-1-84953-242-6

Substantial discounts on bulk quantities of Summersdale books are available to corporations, professional associations and other organisations. For details contact Summersdale Publishers by telephone: +44 (0) 1243 771107, fax: +44 (0) 1243 786300 or email: nicky@summersdale.com.

CONTENTS

INTRODUCTION

They're known as the 'Elephant Years' – when you get to a certain age you turn grey and your ears get bigger. The only difference between you and an elephant is that an elephant never forgets and you never remember anything.

But, as one poem in this book asks, 'How old is old?' Some people are still bungee-jumping in their nineties. Well, some are bungee-jumping and others are tripping down the stairs and getting their braces caught on the banisters – which, as a spectator sport, amounts to pretty much the same thing. And then, we have 'young fogeys' – old before their time, mooching around in flat caps or twinsets and moaning about the state of the world. Yes, being an 'oldie' is really a state of mind, not simply your mind being in a state.

They say that youth is wasted on the young, but then age is wasted on the old. We don't appreciate it. We moan about it and groan about it, we mumble and we grumble about it, when we should of course be embracing it. It comes to us all – if we're lucky. To paraphrase Kipling: If you can meet with youth and age and treat those two impostors just the same then fair dos, good on you and jolly hockey sticks. Because, frankly, while no one wants wrinkles, who wants acne? If you're going to have lines on your face you might as well make sure they're laughter lines. That is what this book is for: to find the 'fun' in 'pension fund', the 'grin' in 'chagrin', and the 'gold' in 'getting old'.

And don't forget: there's always someone older than you are. If you can't laugh at yourself, laugh at them instead.

Remember?

Remember policemen oh-so-polite?
Remember kids well-behaved?
Remember nights out for just ten bob?
Remember the money we saved?

Remember the boys in nice ties and suits?
Remember the girls, young and shy?
Remember the brain cells we once had?
No, neither do I!

TEETH

I can't eat nuts or gobstoppers,
I've got no molars left in my head.
All I can get my teeth into now
Is the glass at the side of the bed.

How Old is Old?

Is it when your fingers feel cold
When everyone else is in shorts?
Or is it when you realise
You're permanently out of sorts?

Is it when you can't hear so well
When one of the family's phoning?
Or when you finally realise
That your favourite hobby is moaning?

Is it the first time you're addressed
As 'granddad' or 'silly old moo'?
Or when you turn on the light three times a night
And shuffle off to the loo?

Is it when you turn sixty-five
Or sixty or fifty or less?
Or when you go to the beach one day
And are too embarrassed to undress?

Or perhaps it's that fateful moment
That always comes too soon,
When you look in the mirror
And come face to face
With a human form of prune.

The optimists say, 'Hey, hey, hey,
Age is all in the mind.'
And the pessimists say, 'Get away, get away,
Age is all in your lines.'

But whatever you say
And whatever you think
And however old you act,
The only thing worse than growing old
Is not growing old – fact!

THE QUEEN
OF THE LIBRARY

I'm the queen of the library,
I get books out every week.
Mills & Boon or Lorna Doone,
Though I baulk at Mervyn Peake.

Give me a good bodice-ripper;
Something to make me wince.
I tell all my friends that when I go to bed
I curl up with my large prints.

Nostalgia

A teapot shaped like a cottage,
An old Dinky toy Austin van,
A Bakelite phone like I used to own
And a model of Superman.

My past life flashes before me,
I see all that I used to know,
Nostalgically, on my TV,
When I watch the *Antiques Roadshow*.

Keeping Fit

Bend those knees! Squat right down!
Now start on lifts! You see?
It's amazing just how fit you'll get
Sitting down for a cup of tea.

WHAT MY PENSION MEANS

P is for 'pitiful',
E is for 'execrable',
N is for 'next to nowt'.
S is for 'spendable',
I for 'indefensible', hardly worth taking out.
O is for 'Oh dear, we're right up the creek',
N is for 'nothing left' by the end of the week.

CONTEMPLATION ON BECOMING A HUNDRED

I'm looking forward to becoming a hundred
And my telegram from the Queen,
Or an email or text or whatever comes next,
If you know what I mean.

I'll treat myself to a brand-new hat –
Maybe even a fur one.
But when the Queen's waiting for her telegram
Who on earth is going to send her one?

A Fruity Poem

An apple a day keeps the doctor away
They say, if you aim it correctly,
It seems to form a perfect arc
With a beautiful trajectory.

You can use one on your other half
If you should catch them kipping
When they've promised to tidy, cook or clean –
Oh bless the Cox's Pippin!

And when the family all come round,
Even though they're kin and kith,
You can see them off at bedtime
With a well-aimed Granny Smith.

'What's that? What's that, behind your back?'
They ask, all sort of suspicious,
Surely to goodness they wouldn't think
You're concealing a Golden Delicious?

And if the apple bowl runs out
You could chuck a rotten tomato,
Or the ultimate oldie WMD:
A rock-hard King Edward potato.

PILLS

I have six blue pills with my breakfast
And nine yellow ones with my tea,
Then thirty-two more with my cocoa
And that's why I rattle, you see.

My husband takes more than I do,
It really drives us crackers.
You can hear us coming down the road
Like a pair of flippin' maracas!

THE NIGHT-TRIPPER

I used to be up half the night,
At parties, having fun,
But now I'm up half the night
On the toilet run.

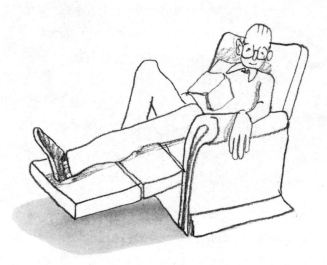

HOME COMFORTS

There's a very good way to gauge
If you've reached 'a certain age',
Home comforts mean much more
When you get home and shut the door.

A lovely cup of tea (and cake!)
Just like mother used to make,
Remote control poised to zap
And a curled-up cat upon your lap.

Heaven, bliss, and sheer nirvana
Housework can wait, *mañana, mañana.*

THE WONDROUS STAIRLIFT

Stairs can be a problem,
When you're getting on a bit.
No leaping up two at a time
Like when you were young and fit.

But then there came the stairlift,
Which is really, really clever.
Now I'm whizzing up the stairs
Even faster than ever.

HERE IS THE NEWS

Hold the front page, stop the press,
I've lost my jigsaw piece!
Tell them on the *News at Ten*
That I've spilt cocoa on my fleece!

Call Downing Street to let them know
I've bust my reading specs;
Inform the US president:
We've found new wrinkles on our necks.

Tell the United Nations
To send peacekeepers to my house,
I'm being pelted with crockery
By my ever-loving spouse!

It's one thing after another
When you reach a certain age,
So send the newsmen all round here
And HOLD THE FRONT PAGE!

HAIR, THERE AND EVERYWHERE

When hubby hit his forties
His hair began to go.
He tried all sorts of potions
To see if it would grow.

Castor oil, bird poo, varnish –
Nothing did the trick.
We thought we'd never see again
His hair all long and thick.

But now he's hit his sixties,
His hair just grows and grows.
The only little drawback is
It's from his ears and nose.

MY MOBILITY SCOOTER

It's got go-faster stripes
And awesome power,
It does nought to twenty
In half an hour.

I race down the pavement
Without a sound –
No one's safe
With me around.

Scooter technology is
So far advanced
Even kids on their skateboards
Don't stand a chance.

They hide in the doorways
Of fast-food joints;
Running down hoodies
Gets me fifty points!

You can keep your car racing
On your home computer,
I get my kicks
On my mobility scooter.

THE WORLD CHAMPION
KNITTER

Pay attention now, don't you titter,
I am the world's champion knitter.
For my husband I've knitted socks
And when he went bald I knitted dreadlocks.

My boiled eggs and teapots all have cosies
And the kittens have mittens to warm their toesies.
My son, the biker, has a woolly crash hat
So he'll have a soft landing, I made sure of that.

I made a bulletproof vest for the local bobby,
Though the bulk made him look like Mr Blobby.
And if the Queen should happen to call
There's a knitted red carpet out there in the hall.

There's nothing – but nothing – that I can't knit,
As long as I've got a pattern for it.
And if my family fall under a train
I'll knit some replacements, two pearl, one plain.

Olympian Locks

My hair was once blonde
And then it turned grey,
And then, bit by bit,
It all went away.

A bit like a runner,
Or so I've been told,
My hair deserves medals:
Bronze, silver and old.

IDENTITY CRISIS

Yesterday I forgot who I was –
Was I the Duke of Beaumont?
Or the Queen of Sheba or Donald Duck?
Or was it my first senior moment?

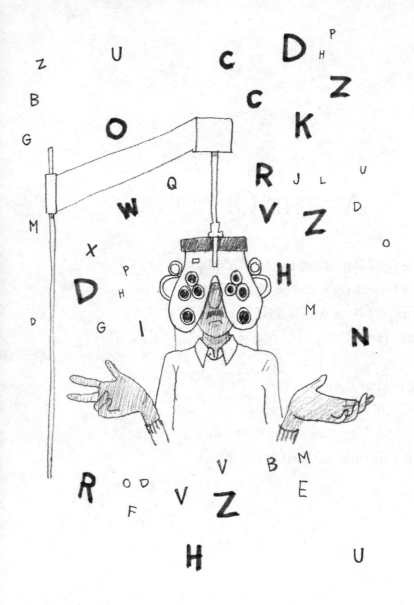

AT THE OPTICIAN'S

The optician asked me to read aloud
The letters up there on the wall,
I saw a J – or was it a K?
You know, I can't see bugger all.

He said at the end, 'That's fifteen "fails",
And only a couple of passes.
Now we'll try once more, if you don't mind,
But this time *without* your glasses.'

NEIGHBOURHOOD WITCH

Peeking through the curtains,
She sees your every move.
Thin-lipped and inscrutable,
Like that portrait in the Louvre.

She watches all your visitors
As they come and go;
If she had a pound for every one
She'd be rolling in the dough.

She makes notes in her diary
And sometimes calls the law,
Though by the time that they get round
She forgets what she's called 'em for.

She's a flipping nuisance –
She thinks she's Sherlock Holmes,
And where was she when someone swiped
My favourite garden gnomes?

You think she'd have something better to do
Than peering through her nets.
She's probably hoping to catch someone
Parading in just their kecks.

So how do I know so much about
The old bat at twenty-three?
Well, round the clock, without a stop
I watch *her*, you see!

An Oldies' Valentine

Roses are red,
Violets are blue,
We're too old for sex,
So let's have a brew!

HOUSE-PROUD

I like to dust my nick-nacks
Before people come to tea,
I like the house all spotless,
As perfect as can be.

There's a place for everything
And everything in its place,
Apart, of course, from my dear hubby
Who's a permanent disgrace.

Busy doing nothing,
Shirt tail all a-flap,
Stubble where he's missed a bit,
Crumbs nestling in his lap.

He looks a proper shocker,
Like something from the ark,
And like a human lighthouse
He even stands out in the dark.

When I sweep the specks of dust
Under the rug in the loo,
Would it be OK, just for today,
If I swept him under too?

Drinking And Driving

When we go out on the town,
I make my hubby drive.
It's good to know you'll get home again,
Let alone arrive.

Then I can let my hair down
And come home, face all pink.
When all's said and done, in more ways than one,
That man really drives me to drink.

Why It's Great
To Be Old

When you get to a certain age
You can say and do what you think.
They'll just say you're a 'character',
With a bit of a nudge and a wink.

You can be rude to all the salesmen
When they come and call;
You can call them all the names you like
From the safety of your hall.

And though everyone else is taller,
They have to look up to you.
At a venerable age you're deemed a sage
Whatever you say or do.

You can stand out on the high street
And embarrass teenyboppers,
By swearing at the top of your voice
And saying 'knickers' to the coppers.

You can get away with anything
When you reach a certain age.
As soon as you think you're past it
You're just at the perfect stage.

So put your clothes on back to front
And giggle like a loon,
If you weren't a pensioner
You'd be in a padded room.

Say what you like, say what you think,
It really doesn't matter,
When you get to the point you should know better
You can be as mad as a hatter.

ELVIS

If Elvis were alive
He'd be over seventy-five
And might not have all his hair.
A bald Elvis sounds shocking
And would he still be rocking?
Probably just in his chair.

BIRTHDAYS

Every year my birthday
Comes round a little quicker;
No wonder I drown my sorrows
In soft-centres and hard liquor.

And the price of the birthday candles
Is getting out of hand,
I've had to resort to the supermarket's
Cheapo-cheapo brand.

Soon there'll be another milestone,
Ninety – flippin' heck!
Not so much a milestone
As a millstone round my neck.

Though, when you reach your middle age
You wonder what's to toast.
But when you're over ninety,
That's when you can start to boast!

THE PENSION POLICE

Don't you know it's against the rules
To use your bus pass for pub crawls?
It simply wasn't meant for pubbing,
Even less to go nightclubbing.

And one other thing we should mention:
Don't get drunk on your old-age pension.

TV MEMORIES

Ooh look, there's what's-his-name
Who used to be on *The Bill.*
Or was it *Morse,* or *Sherlock Holmes*
Or Maybe *Benny Hill?*

I know his face, it'll come back to me
Oh, what's his flippin' name?
He used to host *The Golden Shot*
Or was it *The Generation Game?*

When you've watched TV
for so long, since 1952,
You'll find your whole past TV life
Can flash in front of you.

There's what's-his-face from *Take Your Pick*
And her from *Fawlty Towers,*
Oh, what's her name? This guessing game
Could last for hours and hours.

Look! She's the one off thingummybob,
Who used to be married to him,
And didn't he get a CBE
In the New Year's honours thing?

And that one there, without the hair
He used to present the footie.
And the one behind the one in front
Didn't he have a hand in *Sooty*?

And wasn't he a Doctor Who
Back in the mists of time?
Or a TV cook, or Captain Hook
Or that show where they used to mime?

The names of every TV star
Are stored in my memory bank,
But when I try to recall them
My mind goes blankety blank.

TAKING STOCK

My jumpers are bobbly,
My knees are knobbly,
And my backside's rather wobbly.

I've got to the stage
Where I quite like beige
Not by choice – it's called old age.

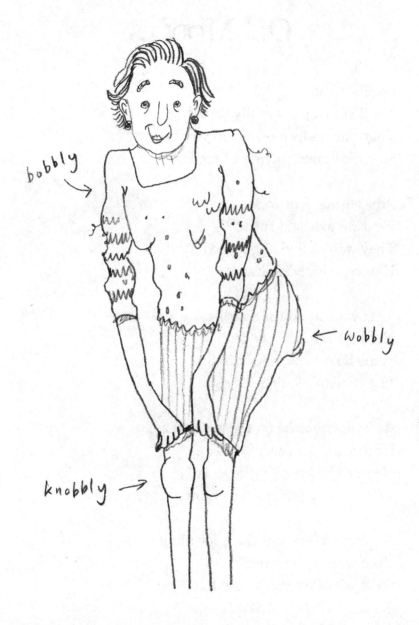

bobbly

← wobbly

knobbly →

OL' MODELS

I'd like to be a model
No, don't laugh, I really would.
They have oldie models too you know,
So, who knows, perhaps I could.

Advertising dentures,
Hearing aids and specs,
They won't mind about the models
Having crinkly necks.

That woman on the stairlift,
Her hair is snowy white;
Some buxom blondie bimbo
Just wouldn't look quite right.

And the old bloke on the pension ad,
He's no kid for sure;
He must be knocking seventy,
Who knows, per'aps even more.

So, there's hope out there for all of us
Who want to be a model,
Strut whatever you've got left
Go on – it'll be a doddle!

A STRIMMERICK

There was an old man called Piers,
Who had the hairiest ears,
But he got satisfaction
When he took drastic action
With a strimmer and very sharp shears.

THE BEAR FACTS

Whenever people say I'm old
I know just what to do,
I say, 'I'm younger than Rupert Bear
And also Winnie the Pooh.'

They were born in the twenties,
And they may be cartoon bears,
But, by my calculations,
They've been drawing their pensions for years!

DECISIONS, DECISIONS, DECISIONS

Shall I take my brolly?
Should I wear my hat?
Shall I buy new glasses?
Should I get a cat?

Decisions, decisions, decisions,
It really drives me loco.
When someone asks, 'Coffee or tea?'
My hubby says I should cocoa.

PUBLIC LOOS

I've searched all down the high street,
The alleyways and mews,
But where oh where, oh where oh where
Oh where are the public loos?!

Many's the time I've sworn and shouted,
Many's the time I've cussed,
Trying to walk cross-legged,
And bursting, fit to bust.

Once, oh not so long ago,
There'd be gents' and ladies' too,
So whose bright idea was it then
To phase out the public loo?

I've searched in vain for toilets
And sadly not found any,
So what do you do without a loo
When you want to spend a penny?

They should have 'em in the supermarkets
And offer loyalty points,
But in the meantime, thank the Lord,
For the ones in the fast-food joints!

MIRROR, MIRROR

Mirror, mirror on the wall
What's this I see before me?
Wrinkled skin, grey wisps of hair –
Someone reassure me.

I was young and pretty once
At least I think I was, you know,
And maybe that's why Mother Nature
Makes your memory go.

FOOD FOR THOUGHT

Peanut butter's fattening,
Jam and marmalade too.
What should I put on my toast, then?
What is a girl to do?

When you're that little bit older
Nothing goes to waste,
Every crumb devoured and more
Though it seems to collect at your waist.

I'll invent a low-fat alternative
To put on toast and bread:
Low on cals, big on taste,
I could call it my 'Middle-Age Spread'!

HOSPITAL

Hospitals, hospitals, hospitals –
I'm in one every week,
For check-ups and tests,
And all the rest,
Now everything's started to creak.

Me hips, me knees, and if you please
All me bits and bobs,
Are examined by lots
Of nurses and docs,
Still, it keeps 'em all in jobs.

And the car parks cost me a fortune;
You'd think that when you're older
They'd let you in free
Or at least let you be
A season ticket holder.

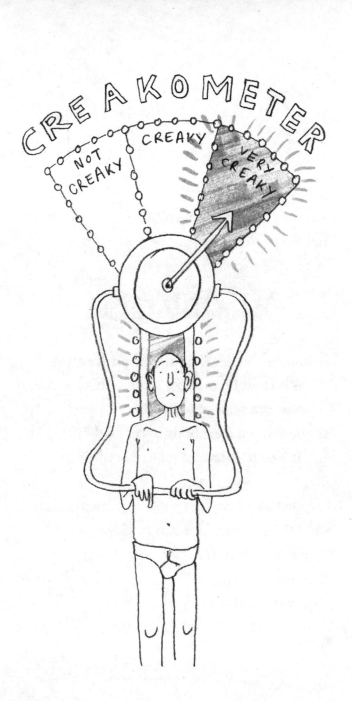

ALE AND ARTY

There was an old man called Dearing,
Who had lost almost none of his hearing,
The exception it seemed
Was when somebody screamed
'It's your turn to get the beer in!'

BRITAIN'S SAFEST DRIVER

I really don't like to boast,
But I'm the driver with the most.
From John o'Groats to Cornwall,
I've toured Britain coast to coast.

A perfect, spotless licence
For fifty-something years,
A prang or two, that much is true,
When I was caught unawares.

You can keep your souped-up sports cars,
With all their speed and power,
Why on earth should you need to exceed
Fifteen miles an hour?

Out on the open road, carefree,
That's where you'll always find me.
And by some brilliant stroke of luck
The traffic jam's always behind me.

I never booze, though I sometimes snooze
At the wheel for a moment or two,
But not for long as I have to wake up
And stop to find a loo.

I'm probably the safest driver
In the fastest or slowest lane,
So I can't understand why they're asking me
To take my test again.

HELPING THE AGED

Can you please unscrew this jar for me?
Can you help me across the road?
Can you please give up your seat for me?
Can you carry this heavy load?

Can you speak a little louder please?
Can you let me jump the queue?
It's great when you're old
They all do as they're told
It's one of the perks, thank you!

My New Interests

I've got quite hooked on gardening
And rambling's now a must.
I even care about stocks and shares
And I've joined the National Trust.

I buy my shoes for comfort,
Don't care about the trends.
I don't 'get' the Internet,
I write letters to my friends.

And as for modern music,
Rap was the last straw.
I'd rather listen to *The Archers*
On good old Radio 4.

I suppose all this makes it obvious
I'm no longer quite so young.
But in secrecy, between you and me,
Being older is much more fun.

A Bit of What You Fancy

A bit of what you fancy
They say will do you good,
A drink or two and chocolate too
And a piece of your favourite pud.

But why stop there, I ask myself?
Why follow it to the letter?
A lot of what you fancy
Will surely do you better.

Poor Old Rover

I feel sorry for old Rover,
He's really past his prime.
Taking him for walkies now
Takes more than twice the time.

Even throwing sticks for him
Is no good for my health,
He just sits there looking stupid
And I fetch them all myself.

He's got pills for this, pills for that
He's always down the vets.
He's costing me a fortune –
Who'd have flippin' pets?

He's not as old as me you know
He's only in his teens,
Though work it out in dog years
And he's one of life's has-beens.

Still, I'll tend and care for him
Until he pops his clogs
Unless of course there's such a thing
As an old-folks' home for dogs.

OLDIES' OLYMPICS

They should have Olympic Games
For oldies with their walking frames.
The marathon could be completed
Within three months, but not repeated.

The javelin they could amend
For walking sticks with sharpened ends.
The long jump would be even sweeter
A new world record – ten millimetres!

The tug-of-war would be worth a look:
Teams tugging on a pension book.
The swimming would not be forgotten:
First pensioner to reach the bottom!

Oh, if only they would have some games
For oldies with their walking frames!

Sixteenth Birthday

I was born Feb twenty-ninth
But mum forgot to mention,
That by my sixteenth birthday
I'd be due my old-age pension.

Golden Oldie

When I went bald I bought a blonde wig,
To help me smile and cheer up.
But now, instead of 'Baldilocks',
I'm known as 'Golden Syrup'!

DUNMOANIN'

Why is it, when some folk retire,
They move down to the sea?
Frankly, that's the very last place
I would want to be.

Being old and distant
Will only make people say,
'Why on earth are my old friends
Over the hill and far away?'

Senile Delinquents

Wearing leather cardies
And Doc Marten carpet slippers,
They sit around on street corners
Shouting at the nippers.

Revving up their scooters,
Mobility ones of course,
They try to put the wind up
The terrified police force.

These old senile delinquents
They always get their kicks,
By brandishing their weapons:
Sawn-off walking sticks.

The Land Of Myopia

I live in the land of Myopia
Where all is permanently blurred.
If I saw a flying pig
I'd probably think it was a bird.

If a saucer full of Martians
Landed down my street,
I'd probably think they were mending the road
And make cakes for them to eat.

If my house were being watched
By spies from the CIA,
I'd think they were trick-or-treating
And give them sweets to go away.

So why don't I buy some glasses
I hear you say from afar,
Well, the truth you see, is I've got some
But I just can't see where they are!

A Short Poem

I used to be six-foot-three,
With a military bearing to boot,
But somehow now I'm four-foot-ten
And they've had to alter my suit.

Was it due to smoking?
Or drinking, or a bit of both?
Or could it be that ageing
Is the thing that stunts your growth?

TEENYBOPPER SHOCK

I've lived in some denial,
I've been refusing to admit,
That OK, come on, I'll say it,
I'm getting on a bit.

I've used up countless potions
To keep the years at bay,
Botox for the wrinkles,
Hair dye for the grey.

My teeth have all been whitened,
I wear quite trendy clothes.
I've even had some surgery
On my ancient crooked nose.

But last week in the salon
I had quite a shock,
Flicking through a magazine
They had a piece on rock.

A pin-up from my teenage years,
A prince of teenybop,
Had wrinkles and a long grey beard
'OK,' I said, 'fair cop.'

I'm officially quite old now,
It's that teenybopper's fault.
The big secret of ageing
Is get older, but don't get caught!

MY WALKING STICK

My walking stick's a weapon,
It's my AK-47.
Don't you dare try mugging me
Or you'll be history.

And if I see a hold up,
Before the cops have rolled up,
I'll stop a fleeing villain
Like the Wild West's Matt Dillon.

I'm like that *Avengers* feller,
John Steed with his umbrella,
Foiling fiends and foes
With a swift crack on the nose.

The only problem with this thing
Is when I take a swing;
There is a certain lack of grace
When I fall flat down on my face.

AN OLDIE NURSERY RHYME

Jack Sprat can eat no fat
His wife can eat no lean.
Since they got their pensions
They can't afford to eat a bean.

OLD-FASHIONED CURSES

Damn and blast! Blast and damn!
These old expressions show that I am
Not a whippersnapper now –
There I go again, silly cow!

You have to watch just what you say,
It really gives the game away.
These old expressions from the past
Will show your age – damn and blast!

WHEELCHAIR RACES

They say that in certain places
Oldies have wheelchair races.
The wheelies and jumps
And astonishing stunts
Put the smiles right back on their faces.

GOING, GOING, GONE

I'm confused
Well, aren't you?
The high street's now been
Built anew.

The bank's a pub,
The pub's now flats,
Woolies a pound shop
Selling tat.

Estate agents galore
And charity shops –
Coffee bars?
Yes, lots and lots!

Greengrocers, butchers
All disappeared,
Town hall too,
That's been cleared.

    Even the church
    Is now a bar:
    'Holy Joe's',
    That's one step too far.

        I'm too old
        For this toing and froing,
        It's not my memory
        It's my past that's going!

Senior Sex Symbols

The missus goes moony
Over that George Clooney,
I just don't get it at all.
He's over fifty, just like me
And his hair's greyer than mine an' all!

THE POP STARS
OF OUR YOUTH

The pop stars of our youth
Have never gone away,
They've carried on regardless
Whether bald or grey.

Rocking out at stadiums
Where we all sing along,
To all their hits of yesteryear
Now, they were proper songs.

You can keep your indie.
Acid house and rap.
The only decent modern band
Is that lot Spinal Tap.

Back then it was decent lyrics:
Um, um, um or fa, fa, fa,
'Hi ho silver lining',
De do-do-do, de da-da-da.

The only drawback of these bands,
These mothers of invention,
To see 'em costs a hundred quid,
A whole week's old-age pension!

MATURE

Mature's a polite word for getting old,
But if you're a cheese you start to grow mould
'Vintage' sounds better, like a fine wine,
I won't ask your age, if you don't ask mine.

NEW TECHNOLOGY

Mobile phones, pads and pods,
It's all beyond my ken.
My idea of a word processor
Is a proper fountain pen.

People say I'm behind the times
But I don't bloomin' care.
To me the Net's for catching fish
Or something you put on your hair.

And when the government announced
PCs in every school,
I thought they meant some coppers
To help enforce the rules.

See, up to now I've got on fine
Without technology,
Well, apart from my plans for a gastric band
And a new bionic knee.

OUR GENERATION

People try to put us down
Just because our hair ain't brown,
Because we have some wisps of grey
They wish that we would go away.

We were once quite young like you
We liked the Beatles and the Who,
We didn't always look this way
But like Visage we fade to grey.

So nice to be forever young
Like in that song that Dylan sung,
But getting older's not a crime
And like Cher we can't turn back time.